**Practice writing your name.
Draw a picture of yourself.
The book belongs to:**

ME

CAPITAL LETTERS
Trace the capital letters.

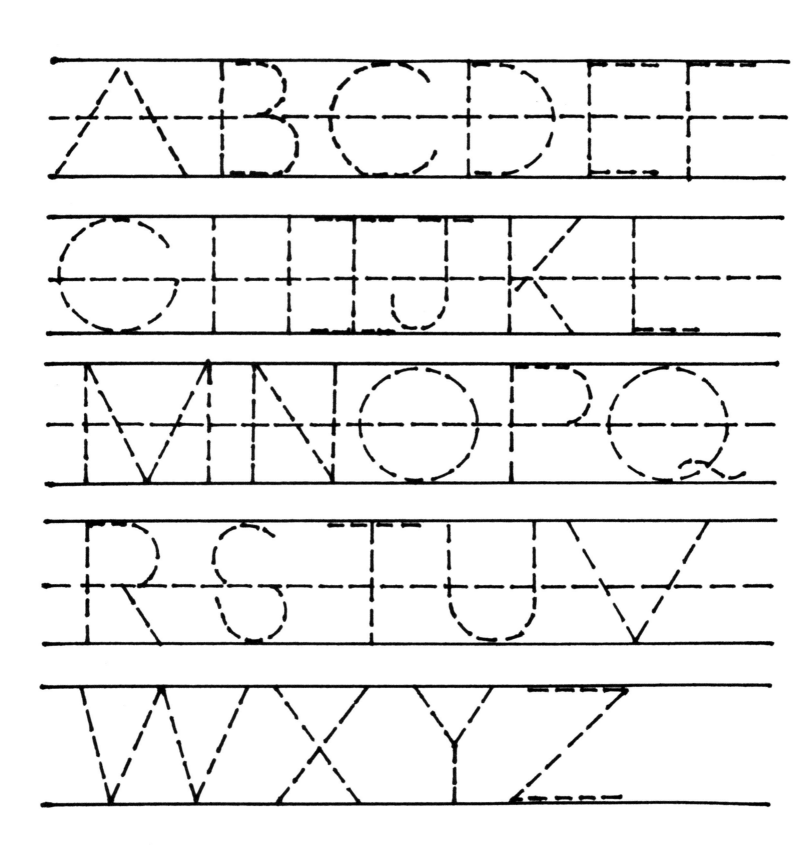

Practice writing the letters yourself.

SMALL LETTERS
Trace the small letters.

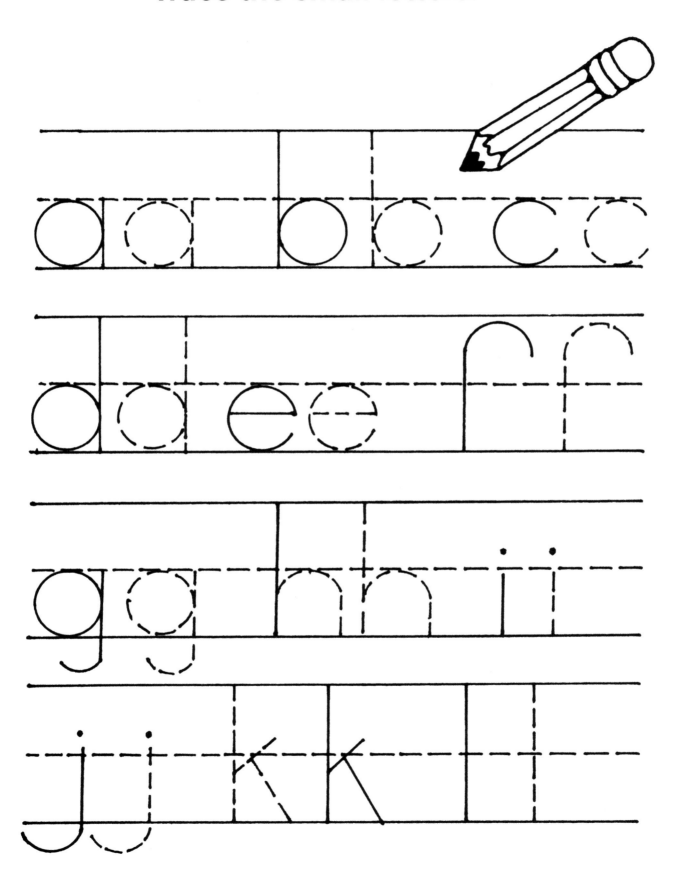

Practice writing the letters yourself.

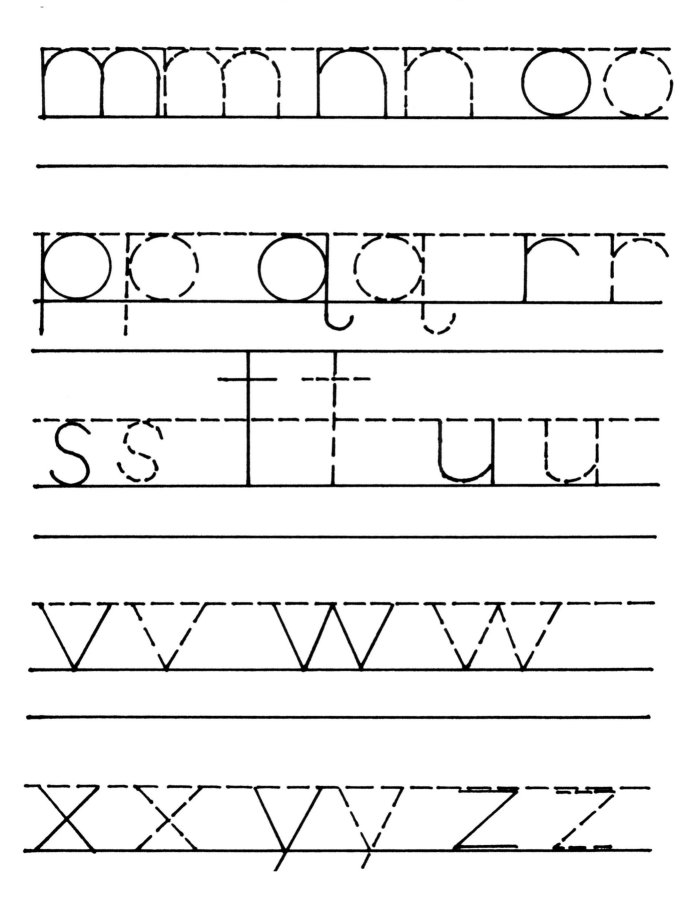

Trace the capital and small letters.

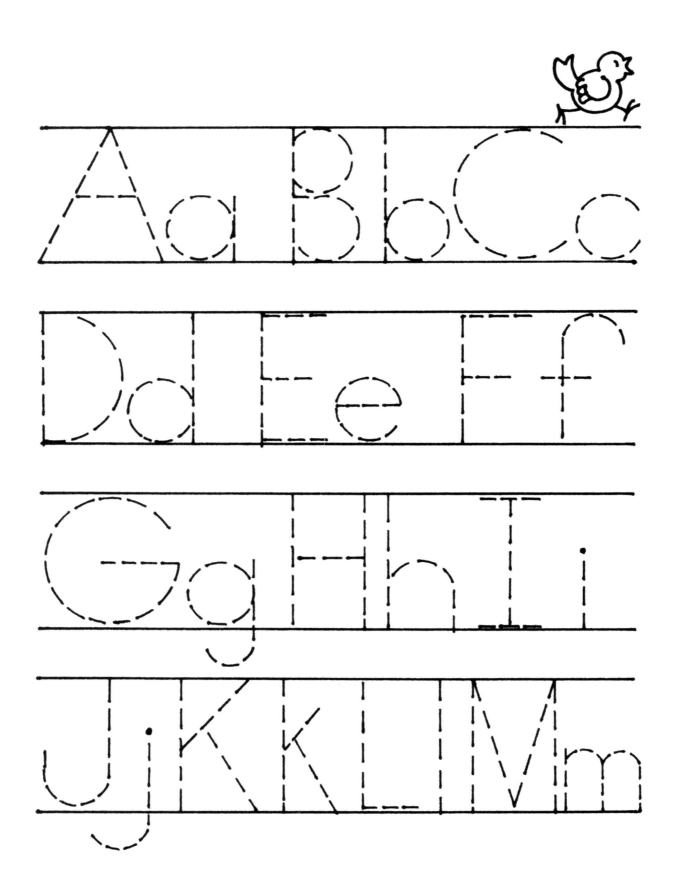

Nn Oo Pp

Qq Rr Ss Tt

Uu Vv Ww

Xx Yy Zz

Draw a line from the capital letter to the matching small letter. The first one is done for you.

A — b	E — g
B — a	F — e, h
C — d	G — h
D — c	H — f

I — k	M — n
J — l	N — o
K — j	O — m
L — i	P — p

Q — q	V — y
R — s	W — z
S — r	X — w
T — u	Y — x
U — t	Z — v

These capital and small letters are all mixed up. Draw a line from the capital letter to the small letter that matches it.

a •	m	B •	• t
G •	A	H •	• b
M •	S	n •	• h
s •	g	T •	• N

F •	u	C •	• v
i •	O	l •	• R
o •	l	r •	• L
U •	f	V •	• c

d •	D	E •	• p
K •	w	J •	• X
q •	Q	x •	• e
W •	Y	P •	• j
y •	k	z •	• Z

The vowels are A E I O U (and sometimes Y). Every word has one or more vowels in it. Color the picture using this vowel letter guide.
A Green　　E Yellow　I Blue　O Orange　　U Red

Help the duckling find their mother and father. Fill in the missing letters on the stone path.

Follow the letters to find out who is playing with the alphabet balls.

What word is spelled in the balls?

Say the name of the first thing in the box. The word begins with the letter next to it. Circle the other things in the box that begin with the same letter.

Say the name of the object at the top of the box.
This word begins with the letter near it.
Cross out anything in the box that does NOT begin with this letter.

Ii
inch worm

Jj
jet

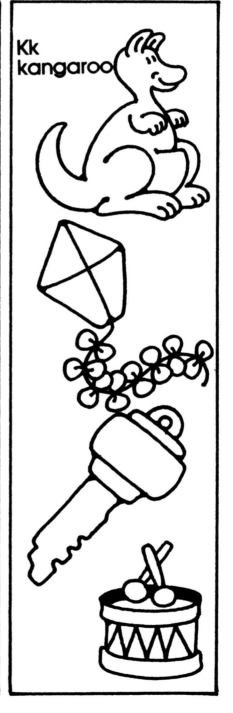

Kk
kangaroo

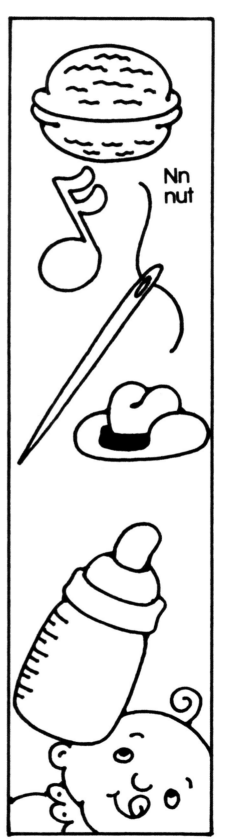

Color the things in each box that begin with the letter in the circle.

Draw a line from the object to the letter that object begins with. The name of the object is printed under the letter.

Zz
Zebra

Yy
Yo-Yo

Xx
xylophone

Ww
watermelon

Say the name of the object on each line. What does this word begin with? Write the capital and small letter for each word.

What words do you know?
Write these words below and then on the signs in the parade on the next page.

Color the letters of the alphabet. Practice saying them as you color.

Try to figure out how to spell the words. Choose a letter that you think makes the word spelled correctly.

__F__ __O__ __G__

____ __R__ __E__ __E__

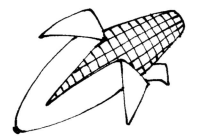

__C__ __O__ ____ __N__

____ __O__ __A__ __T__

Missing letters. Fill out the letters of the alphabet that are missing.

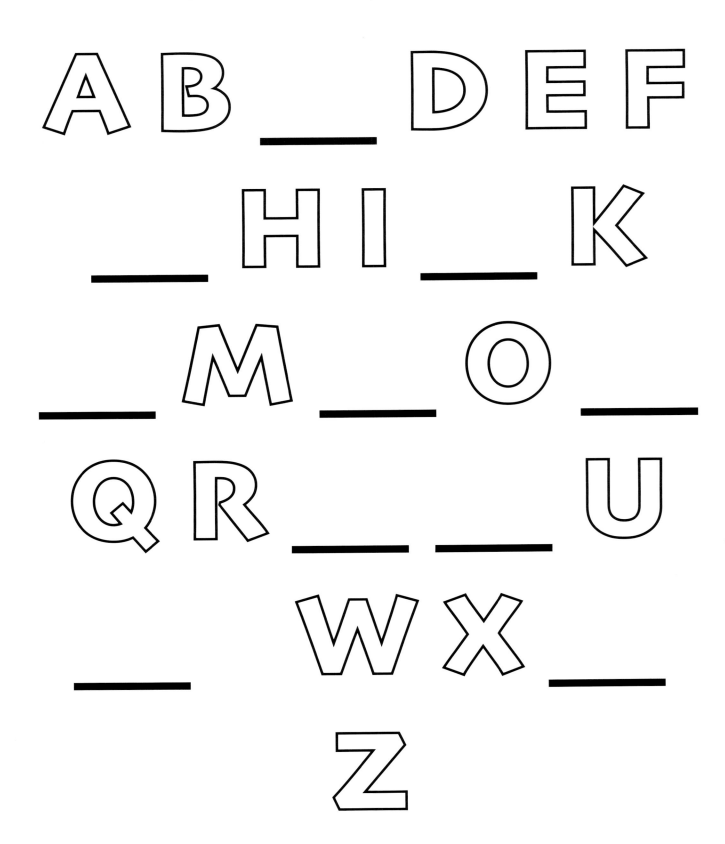

Cross out the letters that are in the wrong order.

Color the letters with a dot and write them on the line below. What does it spell?

___ ___ ___ ___ ___ ___ ___ ___

Look at the picture and figure out what the mixed up letters spell.

__ __ __   __ __ __ __
O G D   H F S I

__ __ __ __   __ __ __
I L N O   T C A

__ __ __   __ __ __ __
G P I   T A G O

Look at the picture and figure out which part of the body the mixed up letters spell.

__ __ __   __ __ __ __
R A M   A H D N

__ __ __ __   __ __ __
O F T O   E T O

__ __ __   __ __ __ __
G L E   E A H D